SPOTLIGHT ON
AN EQUITABLE WORLD

T0284464

FINDING YOUR VOICE FOR HUMAN RIGHTS

Mary Ratzer

ROSEN PUBLISHING

Published in 2025 by The Rosen Publishing Group, Inc.
2544 Clinton Street, Buffalo, NY 14224

Copyright © 2025 by The Rosen Publishing Group, Inc.

First Edition

All rights reserved. No part of this book may be reproduced in any form without permission in writing from the publisher, except by a reviewer.

Editor: Greg Roza
Book Design: Michael Flynn

Photo Credits: Cover Carlo Prearo/Shutterstock.com; cover, p. 3 (hands) Dedraw Studio/Shutterstock.com; (series Earth icon) v4ndhira/Shutterstock.com; p. 5 https://commons.wikimedia.org/wiki/File:Eleanor_Roosevelt_UDHR_(27758131387).jpg; p. 6 Krakenimages.com/Shutterstock.com; p. 7 New Africa/Shutterstock.com; pp. 9, 17 Prostock-studio/Shutterstock.com; p. 10 Ground Picture/Shutterstock.com; p. 11 Hero Images Inc/Shutterstock.com; p. 13 Monkey Business Images/Shutterstock.com; p. 15 Djohan Shahrin/Shutterstock.com; p. 18 CREATISTA/Shutterstock.com; p. 19 Jamie Lamor Thompson/Shutterstock.com; p. 21 fitzcrittle/Shutterstock.com; p. 22 https://commons.wikimedia.org/wiki/File:210120-D-WD757-2704_(50860504153).jpg; p. 23 https://commons.wikimedia.org/wiki/File:210120-D-WD757-2531_(50861220401).jpg; p. 25 https://commons.wikimedia.org/wiki/File:Frederik_de_Klerk_with_Nelson_Mandela_-_World_Economic_Forum_Annual_Meeting_Davos_1992.jpg; p. 26 https://commons.wikimedia.org/wiki/File:Unemployed_men_queued_outside_a_depression_soup_kitchen_opened_in_Chicago_by_Al_Capone,_02-1931_-_NARA_-_541927.jpg; p. 27 https://commons.wikimedia.org/wiki/File:Signing_Of_The_Social_Security_Act.jpg; p. 29 Liv Oeian/Shutterstock.com.

Library of Congress Cataloging-in-Publication Data

Names: Ratzer, Mary Boyd, author.
Title: Finding your voice for human rights / Mary Ratzer.
Description: Buffalo : Rosen Publishing, [2025] | Series: Spotlight on an equitable world | Includes index.
Identifiers: LCCN 2024005882 (print) | LCCN 2024005883 (ebook) | ISBN 9781499477276 (library binding) | ISBN 9781499477375 (paperback) | ISBN 9781499476996 (ebook)
Subjects: LCSH: Human rights--Juvenile literature. | Political participation--Juvenile literature. | Youth--Political activity--Juvenile literature.
Classification: LCC JC571 .R378 2025 (print) | LCC JC571 (ebook) | DDC 323--dc23/eng/20240216
LC record available at https://lccn.loc.gov/2024005882
LC ebook record available at https://lccn.loc.gov/2024005883

Manufactured in the United States of America

Some of the images in this book illustrate individuals who are models. The depictions do not imply actual situations or events.

CPSIA Compliance Information: Batch #CSRYA25. For further information contact Rosen Publishing at 1-800-237-9932.

Find us on

CONTENTS

Chapter One

HUMAN RIGHTS BASICS

Can you make a list of the human rights that everyone deserves? Many nations have worked to list the rights that belong to global or national citizens. Organizations, leaders, and children all have shared their ideas.

Human rights say that we're all born free and equal. We should have the right to an education, a job, a fair wage, ownership of property, free expression of our views, and privacy. We should have the right to gather peacefully, have fair treatment under the law, and marry and raise a family as we choose. The rights to travel, vote in free elections, and to think freely are basic human rights for all people. So are the rights to security, protection from discrimination, and an adequate standard of living.

You can work for rights and freedoms in your community. You can make personal choices that result in respect for all and protection of human rights. This is everyone's responsibility. In the United States and many other places, groups of citizens have joined together to work for human rights. Progress in racial justice, health care, education, and voting rights are examples of these efforts.

Certain offices of the United Nations (UN), including the Human Rights Council, watch out for human rights across the globe and investigate abuse reports. Their role is to protect human rights, empower people, and help governments fulfill human rights for all citizens.

In 1948, the UN adopted a document called the Universal Declaration of Human Rights. This important document was created by a committee led by Eleanor Roosevelt, shown here holding a large copy of the declaration.

Chapter Two

HAVING ENOUGH

As a student and a member of a family, are you aware of having enough, not enough, or more than you need? Having enough is at the heart of human rights. The right to work and earn a living wage is considered a universal human right, one that applies to everyone in the world. The right to education and the right to a home are universal human rights. The right to healthy food and health care and safety from violence are universal human rights. This includes your community and the wider world.

Volunteering in your communituy is one of the best ways to start finding your voice for human rights. How can you help people in need in your community?

When people don't have enough of these basic things, their human rights are denied. You and your family have human rights. These rights belong to your peers and members of your community too. No one can take them away from you. Poverty denies many people in your world their human rights. Everyone has the responsibility to help solve this problem. Everyone has the responsibility to become an active citizen.

Many students just like you have found ways to work for equity and fairness. Organizing and sharing the effort, they've accomplished a lot! Some teens in Texas organized to pay off school lunch debt for other students. Middle school students in another area provided backpacks filled with school supplies for kids who could not afford them. Young citizens of a U.S. town with refugees stepped up to support them. Their work made a positive difference for people denied their rights to basic things.

Chapter Three

REALITY CHECK

In one U.S. high school class, a teacher challenged his students to list their career and lifestyle goals. He asked them to figure out how much it would cost to reach those goals. He also asked them to figure out how much they could earn if they reached their career goals. When they looked into the details, it was a reality check for many in the class.

What if you have goals to have a career, a nice house, a family, and a car? A good education is a great start. That can be the ticket to a job that pays well. The job that pays well is the ticket to more. If you can afford to go to college, you may be able to reach your other goals. Training in a technical job and learning special skills after high school can also launch you into a job that pays well.

What if you have the same goals, but you don't qualify for training or the education you need? Or you have no way to pay for it? Perhaps your school didn't provide enough opportunity or classes to get you ready for the workforce. Perhaps the cost of tuition is out of your reach. What if the money you can make with a high school diploma (or even a college degree) isn't enough to buy a house? Would it be enough to afford an apartment and reliable transportation? Can you support a family? Do you need two jobs, or three? Many people must work more jobs to survive.

Young families often struggle with paying bills and are forced to get more than one job to cover expenses. This can be even more stressful when the jobs only pay minimum wage.

Chapter Four

SHELTER AND HUMAN RIGHTS

The most basic human rights are about survival. You can't live without food, shelter, health care, and work with which to make money. Shelter is a human right. Homelessness in the United States is on the rise, with almost 600,000 people homeless in 2022. Many have faced eviction from their homes after the government cut COVID-19 pandemic protections. Many more people must choose between paying rent and buying food. Some students' performance in school suffers because of frequent moving.

Many people live in poor quality apartments and houses. Common issues such as mold, lead, rodents, crowding, poor air and water quality, lack of heat, lack of electricity, and unsafe buildings affect people's health. They may have to move a lot because of high housing

Habitat for Humanity is a nonprofit organization that relies on volunteers to help build and maintain homes for those in need. Go to www.habitat.org to learn how you can volunteer!

costs and rent. In many places, there are a lack of affordable options. Those who live in older homes may face high costs to maintain them. These costs often go beyond what families can afford. And even if they are newer, poor-quality homes often cost more to heat, cool, and maintain. Some homes may be in unsafe environments. Safety is also a human right.

There are organizations and volunteers that support families in building affordable homes in safe neighborhoods. Many Girl Scouts and Boy Scouts have learned skills to help with these projects. They've been trained in the safe use of power tools and construction basics. Many young people add more than manpower to projects. Some volunteer in the summer to help with housing projects. People just like you help with community cleanup projects, murals, and development of gardens and playgrounds.

Chapter Five

ENVISION A BETTER WORLD

Local and global action for human rights grows from the hope for a better world. What if you could help shape a society where opportunity is fair, needs are met, and diverse communities thrive? What if you and others could solve just one problem by working together? Being able to see what could be is a great starting point. A strong vision is the beginning of turning ideas into real-world change. Your next feelings, though, might be negative. It's important to recognize this problem. Frustration, fear, or anger are normal, but they can feed a feeling of powerlessness. You might feel like these problems must be solved by somebody else. But this can block effort and action. You might be tempted toward apathy, which means walking away and just not caring. You might feel that one person cannot possibly make a difference. But together, people working for change can make big things happen.

Getting past a negative response is part of finding your voice for human rights. It means moving from awareness of the problem to solving the problem. It can mean getting the problem into hands of capable leaders or decision makers. It can mean bringing other voices into the picture. More people can help when brainstorming a plan for action and coming up with a goal. You never know what you can accomplish until you try!

One way to have your voice heard is by attending community meetings. There, you can discuss the changes you would like to see in your community.

Chapter Six

CHILDREN WITHOUT JUSTICE

It can be important to have evidence of injustice. Numbers can be evidence of rights that are denied. We can draw conclusions from the evidence of injustice for the children of the world. You can read about ways the citizens of the world are responding to these injustices. The more you know, the more you can be a voice for action and part of changing the world for the better.

- The United Nations says that 160 million children worldwide are engaged in child labor.
- About 73 million child laborers work in hazardous conditions.
- One of every six children in the world live in extreme poverty, living on about $2.15 a day as of 2023.
- About 468 million children live in conflict zones with many risks to safety and health.
- About 73 million children in Central Africa, East Africa, Southern Africa, and West Africa will die before their fifth birthday from hunger and disease.
- About 78 million children worldwide don't go to school.
- At least 1 million children worldwide are denied their rights in justice systems, especially if they are refugees, suffer mental illness, or are part of a minority group.

UNICEF is an organization that helps children all over the world.

- Many thousands of children are forced to be child soldiers in countries with violent conflicts.
- About half of children with disabilities around the world never get to go to school.
- About 14 million children under five suffer from severe hunger and cannot grow or thrive.
- In developing countries, one in three girls do not finish primary school.
- About 13 million children in the United States live in poverty.
- One in 30 children in the United States are homeless.

Chapter Seven

HUMAN RIGHTS FOR KIDS AND TEENS

Knowing your rights can empower you to live up to your potential. Knowing these rights can also empower you to support the rights of others. The World Health Organization (WHO) connects health and well-being with human rights.

Some of your rights include being safe, supported, and protected. You may still be dependent on others even as you grow more independent. You have the right to be treated fairly and with respect. You can use your voice and take part in society. You have a right to information. You have the right to be heard and to get a response. Your right to education is probably a big part of your life right now. You also have the right to health, rest, and leisure.

Pay attention to the news about the rights of kids like you. Do you know someone who faces violence in their neighborhood? Do people you know have jobs that keep them up late at night or endanger them with unsafe conditions? Do they ever fall asleep in class or cut school? Have you seen discrimination or disrespect affect someone you know? Do you and your friends have what you need?

Pay attention to those around you who may not have their full rights. You yourself may have the same issue. Recognizing this presents you with a challenge to use your rights to be heard and get a response. Solving problems in your own community is important. Working with others to make change happen is powerful.

Some teens need to work to help their families. This can lead to problems in school and other areas of everyday life.

Chapter Eight

YOUR VOICE FOR HUMAN RIGHTS

Citizens of your community and your country can advocate, or speak up, for human rights. Active citizens, including students, speak with their representatives in government. They influence decisions and decision-makers. Young people have spoken up about difficult topics such as school shootings and mental health. Good public officials encourage people to speak up and take part in decision-making. You have the right to use your voice to work for your rights and the rights of others. You have the right to express your views. You have a right to share your thoughts freely.

In many countries around the world, those living with injustice have no right to vote, protest, or even speak out. In a recent survey asking people to name three of their human rights, many could not

Marley Dias, shown here, created the 1000 Black Girl Books campaign when she was in her teens. This campaign got people to donate books with Black female protagonists to libraries. Dias used social media to get word out to the world.

do so. Those living without rights can't always speak for themselves without risking harm. Increasingly, however, young people in the United States have found their voice in speaking up for human rights. Teens with empathy may work for children who've had their rights stolen from them. Children forced to work, girls denied education, and children fleeing war and famine may need help to have their voices heard. Your voice can help.

The right to use your voice to fight for human rights is a precious and powerful thing. It's good to have awareness and tools to communicate your message. Social media can reach a wide audience. Your words can inform and persuade others.

Chapter Nine

HOW YOU CAN HELP: RESPONSIBILITY

The six big ideas of the Universal Declaration of Human Rights aren't just words in a document. These ideas, framed by the United Nations, are a call to everyone to accept responsibility and work for these rights. Ideas can lead to action.

The Six Themes of the Universal Declaration of Human Rights
- dignity and justice
- development and creating better lives for people around the world
- an environment that is safe, clean, and healthy
- the right to be part of your own culture
- rights and responsibilities for all people regardless of gender
- participation in and making decisions about government

How can you work for dignity and justice in your world? Respect is a positive attitude that you choose. Being respectful shows that you recognize the rights, needs, and worth of others. With a respectful attitude, you use empathy and social awareness to honor human dignity and justice.

How can you be responsible for the environment? Understand the ways in which one person can positively impact Earth. Reduce your use of energy and water. Recycle or reuse everything that you can. Reduce the meat in your diet. Plant trees. Pick up litter. Inspire others to do the same.

You can join protests in your community or in other communities when you see the need for change in the world.

How can you participate in decision making by leaders? Use your voice to communicate the need for change. Gather evidence and join with others to get your views heard. You can do this through letters, phone calls, email, and face-to-face meetings.

Chapter Ten

BE THE LIGHT

When Amanda Gorman read her poem "The Hill We Climb" at the inauguration of President Joseph Biden in 2020, she became the youngest inaugural poet in history. As a Black woman, she shared the darkness of racial oppression and the denial of human rights. She spoke for the power to change, as long as we have the courage to work for it She speaks of a "new dawn … as we free it. For there is always light, if only we're brave enough to see it. If only we're brave enough to be it."

Her words show the light of hope through action:

We are striving to forge our union with purpose. To compose a country committed to all cultures, colors, characters, and conditions of man. And so we lift our gaze, not to what stands between us, but what stands before us. We close the divide because we know, to put our future first, we must first put our differences aside.

When she was just 23, Amanda Gorman became the youngest person to read a poem at a presidential inauguration.

Gorman speaks of the light of fairness, justice, and equity. She talks about "the inheritance of the next generation" and how it can be positive or negative depending on our own actions. She writes of the potential of "a wounded world" to become something far better if people come together to work for it. "Being American," she says, "is more than a pride we inherit. It's the past we step into and how we repair it."

Chapter Eleven

AN INSPIRING HERO

People who care can make the difference between hopelessness and dignity and between justice and injustice. Barriers to human rights can be broken by everyday heroes, some of them close to home. Many historic heroes have given others dignity and hope through their actions. Making a difference first depends on seeing injustice. Then it depends on the decision to do something about it.

Nelson Mandela, born in 1918, took heroic action to end a system of racial segregation and oppression in South Africa. This was called apartheid, which means apartness or separation. The ruling white government passed laws to put all people of color into categories. Non-white people had no power even though they were the majority. Laws controlled where they could live, work, and travel. Restricted from white areas, people of color had to have special papers to justify being there. Access to education, health care, and social services was restricted and unequal.

Mandela was brave. He stood up against apartheid. He inspired others to follow him. For fighting for justice and freedom, he was arrested and spent 27 years of his life in prison. Despite personal suffering, Mandela didn't give in to hate. With worldwide support, he was released from prison and succeeded in ending apartheid.

The government put voting rights for all citizens, regardless of race, in place. Mandela did this in an alliance with a former white president of South Africa, F. W. de Klerk. The two of them won the Nobel Peace Prize together. They were human rights heroes who helped restore dignity, hope, and justice for all in their country.

Mandela and de Klerk shake hands at the 1992 meeting of the World Economic Forum in Davos, Switzerland.

Chapter Twelve

CALL TO ACTION ANSWERED

During the Great Depression (1929–1939), the worst economic disaster in the United States so far, about one out of four workers lost their job. Some parents, unable to feed their own children, sent them away to find work. President Franklin D. Roosevelt, who took office in 1933, created many programs to turn the tide of hopelessness. At that time, many people had no help beyond bread lines and begging for food or work. Families did what they could for their family members who were old, sick, frail, jobless, or hungry. But each person had to face the reality that they had no security or guarantee of support.

Many of Roosevelt's government programs helped people find work. Social Security, created in 1935, assured older people of income when they stopped working. The hopeless poverty of the Great Depression was a call to action for the United States to be more responsible for its citizens in times of crisis.

Franklin D. Roosevelt, seated, signed the Social Security Act into law on August 14, 1935.

Since that time, much funding for health care, benefits for those with disabilities, funding for education, and better housing have expanded a national sense that we stand together in our responsibility to each other. Increasingly, civil rights laws were supported by citizens and leaders. Racial injustice could be a loud call to action. The human rights and needs of people living in poverty still challenge us as a nation and are another call to action.

Over the past 100 years or so, many U.S. citizens have accepted a shared responsibility for their fellow citizens. Media, including books, articles, and songs, show a call for change.

Chapter Thirteen

TOOLS FOR A BETTER WORLD

"When we achieve human rights and human dignity for all people, they will build a peaceful, sustainable, and just world." Antonio Guterres, Secretary General of the United Nations, made this prediction about the future of human rights and our shared future as citizens of this world. Indeed, human rights and dignity are the tools to build a better world. To achieve human rights means that we have the tools in our hands to reach peace, justice, and a healthy planet. A peaceful world is not a hungry world. It is not a world where voices of protest are silenced. A peaceful world depends on education, health, freedom, and safety.

The future belongs to your generation. Young people who commit to their role in creating positive change have spoken. They have demanded that the world give them the tools they need to have a future on a planet that is just, peaceful, and sustainable. Greta Thunberg, for example, is a fierce youth activist for her generation. Take to heart the words she shared with leaders and global citizens:

It may seem like we're asking a lot . . . But this is just the very minimum amount of effort that is needed to start the . . . sustainable transition. So you either do this or you're going to have to explain to your children why you are giving up . . . I am telling you that . . . my generation will not give up . . . We are still telling you . . . to act as if you loved your children above all else.

Thunberg, shown here at a demonstration in Stockholm, Sweeden, has become one of the most outspoken youth voices demanding the world take action against climate change.

Chapter Fourteen

SEE THE FUTURE

Can you picture your life in the future? Do you have goals or dreams that will shape the years ahead? Do you have a plan to help you reach those goals? Your education can help you get there. Your parents and your community can help you get there. A home, food, and clothing are important rights. Health care and a healthy environment are important too. Being safe from harm opens many possibilities for success and happiness. These are your human rights. The United Nations says every world citizen has these rights.

What small steps can you take to ensure the rights of others? Can you help others reach their goals and dreams? Many young people can take action (and have) to change things. They've worked to help restore the dignity of other people. They've helped others see their personal worth and potential. They've worked to remove barriers caused by bias and discrimination. It's important to listen and learn as an ally. You can value differences and build bridges using commitment and empathy. Reach out and use your talents to help the community around you if problems arise. Use your voice. Use your creativity. Use your responsible decision making. And as you dream of your future, dream for others as well.

GLOSSARY

advocate: To support a cause or proposal; also, a person who supports a cause.

apathy: A lack of emotion or concern.

discriminate: To treat people unfairly or unequally because of one's thoughts and beliefs.

empathy: The action of being aware of, comprehending, and being sensitive to another's experiences, thoughts, and feelings; also, the ability to share another's emotions.

eviction: The recovery of property through legal processes.

inauguration: A celebration when someone is elected to a political office.

inheritance: Something received from an older relative, often when they pass away.

leisure: Freedom from work or duties.

oppression: Cruel or unjust use of authority or power.

perspective: Point of view.

protagonist: The main character of a story or narrative.

refugee: A migrant person who flees their homeland to escape disaster, persecution, or war.

segregation: The separation of people based on race, class, sex, gender, or ethnicity.

volunteer: To do something without getting paid for it.

INDEX

TITLES IN THIS SERIES

ROSEN
PUBLISHING

ISBN: 9781499477375

9 781499 477375

BECOMING AN
ACTIVE CITIZEN

Mary Ratzer